Here Comes The Cash

A Quick Guide for the

Newly Wealthy

DIANNA MOSES

Copyright © 2016 Dianna Moses

All rights reserved.

ISBN-13: 978-1539102878
ISBN-10: 1539102874

DEDICATION

This book is dedicated to all the people I hope to help avoid costly financial mistakes. It's for the suddenly divorced or widowed that never managed the finances. It's for every professional athlete that worked tirelessly to make it to the top. It's for every lucky lottery winner. And really every person who worked so hard to achieve their dreams only to have them crushed later when their money was gone.

Table of Contents

INTRODUCTION 1
Your Financial Team 4
    Choosing Your Financial Team 4
    How Do You Choose a Financial Professional? 5
    Their Career Stage – Where Are They? 6
    How Long have they been a Financial Professional? 6
    Will a financial designation help me pick a more qualified financial professional? 7
    Wait, so Whaaaat? 9
    Think Long Term 10
    Like Your Financial Professional 10
    Who is Their Ideal Client 11
    The Sales Pitch 11
    Pressured Decisions 12
    Who Needs to be on Your Financial Team 12
Your Investment Style 13
    DIY or Professional? 14
    Can I Manage My Own Money? 15
    You Don't Know What You Don't Know 15
    Emotional Investing 16
    Decide Your Management Style 17
What To Invest In 19
    How to Calculate Annual Returns 20
    What Returns to Expect in the Stock Market 20
Investments and Taxes 24
    Taxes on Stocks 26

- Is 401k a Good Investment? 32
- Employer Contribution Scenarios 33
- Penalties and Restrictions of 401k Plans 35
- Cash 39
- Bonds 39
- Stocks 40
- Property 40
- How Are Your Investments Taxed? 41
- Bank Products 45
- Investments That Participate In The Market 48
- Investments that are Protected from the Market 52
- Investments That Behave Independently of the Market. 54

Financial Worksheets 62
- Understanding Your Financial Attitude 62
- What Does Money Mean To You? 62
- Retirement 63
- Lump Sums of Money 64
- High Wage Earner 65
- Your Lifestyle 65
- Financial Benchmarks 66
- Big Purchases 67
- Who Do You Owe 67
- Past Financial Problems 68
- Special Circumstance 68
- Your Financial Priorities 68
- Money Thoughts 69

ACKNOWLEDGMENTS

Big shout out to the people in my life who have always shown me love. You know who you are. But especially thank you to my brother Paul and my lifelong friend Marty both of whom have been in my corner every step of my wonderful blissful life. Of course, lots of love goes to my Dobermans. Doctor Doom and Handsome Havoc –their unwavering affection helped remind me money doesn't measure wealth.

INTRODUCTION

If you picked up this book I hope it is because you suddenly find yourself overwhelmed with money and are wondering what to do next. It is geared for people new to wealth and wondering what their first steps should be.

This book is educational and is meant for people with little to no financial background. Use this guide as a stepping stone to decide what to do with the money you have, the money you earn, the money you spend and how you can make it work for you.

Although there is a lot of information about the financial field about what to do for retirement or how to pay off your bills there is still a lot of uncertainty about what you need to do when you have a sudden boost of your net worth. Despite having many mainstream financial experts in the media no one is addressing the questions of the newly wealthy. I have had the opportunity to work on Wall Street for big name firms, I've traded equities, options, commodities and currencies. I have also worked in the financial advisory sector with ultra high net worth people to create complex wealth strategies for multi-generational estates and I've worked with people in cash businesses like hair salons, bars, or dry cleaners who generally don't have retirement plans but do have an abundance of cash. With this varied exposure to all types of wealth strategies big and small I found that the people I really like helping are the ones who are new to money. People who suddenly have a windfall of wealth are often overwhelmed especially athletes because their fortune is so public. They are not sure what to do and commonly they choose to do nothing at all. The proverbial putting your money under your mattress may make you feel better when you don't know what to do or who to talk to but there are many better alternatives. This book will help you get a better understanding as to what your next steps are on how to handle your money. My goal is to provide some helpful information to people who are not quite sure what they should be doing with their money, who they should talk to and if they're doing all the right things along the way.

People often find me more approachable than some other people in the financial industry when talking to me about their financial concerns. I believe this is because I have a reputation of speaking plainly to people and spend a lot of time with explanations Sometimes it is not easy to admit when you don't know something that you feel like you should know. The goal of this guide is to give you some information so you feel confident asking questions and making decisions about handling your new wealth.

It never ceases to amaze me that some financial advisors talk down to their clients using industry jargon and complex terms. To often meetings with a financial advisor were long winded on the advisor's part and with very little time spent explaining what the client needs to know or understanding the client's needs. I wanted to create a guide that used regular every day terms, was easy to read and had simple explanations. You will always have people who make themselves feel more important by talking down to others but now you will have a crash course in what they'll be talking about and be armed with questions to ask.

The goal of this guide is to help you find the right people to make up your team and provide you with a guideline on questions to consider before making decisions. Everyone has different goals, tax brackets, earning potential and therefore there is no one solution that is right for all financial plans.

After reading this book you will be loaded with information to help you ask the important questions. Am I spending too much? Is my plan diversified? Am I protected from a market crash? With this book as a guide you will be able to decide your next steps in your financial future. I hope you enjoy reading this and look forward to being a valuable resource to meeting your goals.

Your Financial Team

Choosing Your Financial Team

Before doing anything with your money the first thing you want to do is ask for advice. Unfortunately a lot of people don't have a qualified person to ask for financial advice. Your great aunt Sally may have amassed a lot of wealth but it doesn't mean she's necessarily the best person to talk to about creating a financial plan. Seek consultations from financial professionals but more importantly the right financial professional.

Most commonly when looking for someone to help manage your finances you will need several types of professionals if you have a larger amount of money. No one can be everything to all people. There's a lot of analogies you can use here like a quarterback and special teams, the primary care doctor and cardiologist, infantryman and sniper – but most everyone understands that in complex matters it is important to have a specialist. Your financial advisor is most likely not going to do your taxes. Your accountant is most likely not the person to help setup a trust. Your lawyer probably is not going to make investment recommendations. You get the idea. You want to work with a specialist in each area so you have the best guidance. Especially when you're working with large sums of money.

When you're setting out to create a financial plan depending on the type of people you work with they will all have different approaches. Some only focus on your return on investment, while others only consider tax implications and others will look at your risk or liability. All of these areas need to be considered and working with someone who thinks about the whole picture is critical. Once you find the advisor or advisory firm you're satisfied with, they should be able to provide you recommended attorneys and accountants they've worked with in the past.

How Do You Choose a Financial Professional?

The burning question – how do you choose a good financial professional? Everyone has heard of people being taking advantage of by unscrupulous people in the financial industry. How do you pick a good financial professional to help guide you in creating a sound financial plan?

When you're looking to hire someone to manage your money there are a few areas to consider that can help you choose the right person. Here are some things to think about first.

Their Career Stage – Where Are They?

Ideally you will create a good relationship with your financial professional and will be working with them for many years to come. Because of the baby boomer generation numerous studies show more than 40% of financial advisors are nearing retirement. If your financial advisor has been in the field for 30 years this may be the case. When they bring another experienced associate in to the meetings to work with you it may be because they're winding down their practice and you'll soon be working with the less experienced advisor. If it's a small firm, they may ease your concerns by mentioning their succession plan. If they don't have a plan in place and they're nearing the end of their career it's possible your business won't mean as much to them as someone who is still growing their practice. Think about a financial advisor as you would a doctor – you want one with experience but not one that's been doing it so long they've got one foot out the door.

How Long have they been a Financial Professional?

This question is not as important but certain something to consider. There are amazing training programs available so a young advisor could have a leg up if the work with experienced mentors. Unfortunately, this is not as common as it should be and is something to be aware of when interviewing advisors. Keep in mind, while the advisor may be new to the advisory field, they may have worked in other related fields like banking, insurance or law which could give them an edge over another advisor will more experience. Don't let age be a deterrent as there are plenty of advisors in their late 20s that are great. It is a good sign if an advisor has worked for several years at the same firm as the majority of people who start in the financial advisory field don't last much more than two years. It's worth remembering that many sales people get into financial advisory role as a second or third career so don't assume because someone is in their 50s they have 20 years of expertise in the financial field.

Will a financial designation help me pick a more qualified financial professional?

The answer to that question is yes and no. The Financial Industry Regulatory Authority (FINRA) recognizes and regulates a few of the designations. Some of the designations that are listed on their website are as follows:

AFC - Accredited Financial Counselor

ARPC - Accredited Retirement Plan Consultant

CFP - Certified Financial Planner

CIMA - Certified Investment Management Analyst

CMP - Certified Medicaid Planner

CRC - Certified Retirement Counselor

CRFA - Certified Retirement Financial Advisor

CSA - Certified Senior Advisor

Obviously with that many designations, it isn't a one-size fits all training program. To make it even more complicated there are numerous other designations available to the financial professional. Some designations may be more worthwhile than some others. Some designations are extremely specialized and may be helpful if you need help in that field. A partial list of other designations you may see are as follows:

ATA - Accredited Tax Advisor

CAM - Chartered Asset Manager

CASL - Chartered Advisor for Senior Living

CDFA – Certified Divorce Financial Analyst

CEA - Certified Estate Advisor

CEBS - Certified Employee Benefit Specialist

CEP - Certified Estate Planner

CFC - Certified Financial Consultant

CFM - Certified Financial Manager

ChFC - Chartered Financial Consultant

CIMC - Certified Investment Management Consultant

CRPC - Chartered Retirement Planning Counselor

CRPS - Chartered Retirement Plans Specialist

CTEP - Chartered Trust and Estate Planner

CWM - Chartered Wealth Manager

FSCP - Financial Services Certified Professional

MFP - Master Financial Professional

RFA - Registered Financial Analyst Designate

RICP - Retirement Income Certified Professional

So with a couple dozen designations floating around it is hard to tell if someone knows what they're doing or not. In lieu of designations another alternative is to perform a FINRA broker check. Depending on the type of firm the advisor is working for and what types of investments they deal with they may not have taken a Series 6 or 7, but it's worth checking. This is also the site that will allow you to see if they've had any incidents reported while they were licensed. Not all financial professionals need these types of licensures as it depends on what types of investments they provide.

FINRA's Rules & Resources portion of their website reminds people "...be aware that Financial Analyst, Financial Adviser (Advisor), Financial Consultant, Financial Planner, Investment Consultant or Wealth Manager are generic terms or job titles, and may be used by investment professionals who may not hold any specific credential."

Wait, so Whaaaat?

Yes, you read correctly. The three things that you'd think really matter, may or may not be that significant. You might hire an advisor with 30 years of experience that is just going through the motions until they retire or you could hire someone in their 20s who has great mentors that does a fantastic job. There's so many designations that it's hard to decide what really matters to you and your needs. So while the above areas are important to consider (experience, age and specialized training) they're not the only factors that need to go into the decision making process.

If you think of your financial professional as a relationship you're starting it may help you make a more informed choice. Choose a financial professional you like and that you feel you can trust. A financial plan is a customized, specific way to meet all of your objectives as they change over your lifetime. You want to be able to count on the advisor to understand your needs and provide solutions that meet your goals.

Think Long Term

When deciding whether to work with someone or not, remember this will be your financial consultant for years to come. This isn't like hiring someone for a one-time deal like painting your house, your advisor should know your current situation, goals and objectives for today and your long term future. If you get the impression your potential advisor plans to retire in the next couple years, they may not be a good fit for you.

Like Your Financial Professional

Your financial plan is something that evolves with you as your life changes. If you don't like your financial professional, you may be less likely to alert them when you have had a big change in your life. If you don't trust the person or feel like they're pressuring you, keep looking. If you don't think you could stand talking to the advisor your interviewing on a regular basis, then definitely keep looking. You need to be comfortable communicating when your situation or objectives change. Also do you get the sense they would contact you if the market conditions change? If they're difficult to reach or you can't get on their calendar you want to find out how often they want to meet for reviews. If you have a large sum of money, every 90 days is very reasonable.

Who is Their Ideal Client

If your financial professional primarily works with mid-level executives with young families, they may not be able to handle the complex strategies of a professional athlete's estate or the divisions of assets in a high net worth divorce. Conversely if your financial professional typically only works with people with a net worth of $10M and above, and you're sitting at $2M, it's possible they won't value your business as highly as their other clients.

In summary, your ideal financial advisor will be a person that has enough experience that they won't be switching careers anytime soon and are knowledgeable, personable, listen carefully, take notes and you like them. If you can put checkmarks next to those categories, you're doing great.

Once you have found a couple of candidates to handle your windfall of wealth what's the next step before signing on as a client? Everyone has different personalities, goals and needs so there's no right answer but you will want to understand what approach works best for meeting your objectives and you will want to know what to expect when working with that advisor.

The Sales Pitch

Your financial advisor will be selling something. The question is are they selling you products or are they selling you the services they can provide? If the advisor is product-driven, they may not have the best product for you. Often these types of advisors use their products to fit your needs rather than finding the best product for you. The advisor who is learning about you, your needs, goals and lifestyle is the one who is looking to create a financial plan tailored to you. Advisors that sell their services and expertise rather than a specific product are usually a better choice for high net worth individuals.

Pressured Decisions

In general, if you're meeting a financial professional for the first time and they want you to sign something right away, it's probably best to walk away. Most advisory firms don't have you signing on the dotted line until they've offered some solutions for your financial needs. The advisor should not be pressuring you into making decisions right away unless you have a time sensitive matter that you're trying to resolve. Don't feel pressured. Remember it is your financial plan, ask questions, understand the path to your objectives and make sure you and your advisor are on the same page.

Who Needs to be on Your Financial Team

How complex and varied your financial team's expertise is will depend on you're the size of your estate and objectives. A comprehensive financial plan will have a trust to protect your estate, it will focus on the tax treatments of your investments and your long term financial strategies. Your financial advisor should work with your estate attorney, your business attorney, your accountant and your insurance agent if your advisor doesn't handle insurance strategies.

Your Investment Style

Once you've chosen a financial professional to work with to manage your money the next step is to determine how much of your money do you want to turn over to your new financial advisor. There are a number of approaches you can take with your new found wealth. This book is geared towards people new to money so the scenarios are geared to people who don't currently have a financial advisor or financial plan in place.

A common but misguided approach to new wealth is that instead of choosing one advisor, they will choose several. The thought process is that they will wait and see how each advisor does over the next year and then move the money to the best one. This approach rarely works for two reasons.

1. Once a decision is made, people are reluctant to follow up with reviews and analysis. They leave the money there whether it's a loss or a gain and put the decision of moving or staying off to some arbitrary date that rarely comes until something drastic happens.
2. Spreading your wealth among multiple advisors rarely provides diversification. Most advisors do a lot of the same basic things so using this method will usually result in redundancy of fees, too much of your money exposed to market volatility and a lack of understanding of your overall portfolio performance.

Reluctance to trust someone with your wealth is expected. However, if you been though your due diligence in choosing your financial professional as discussed in the previous chapter you should feel more confident moving forward. Rather than duplicating your plan with multiple advisors, you can use a smaller portion of your money initially with your advisor. Being honest with your advisor by saying you don't want to sign over your entire net worth will not be offensive. Trust is earned and this is a long term relationship. Talk about a graduated increase in investments. It is important to create a timeline for adding more money to your portfolio otherwise it's human nature to do nothing at all and your money will not be working for you.

DIY or Professional?

Depending on your style you may want to manage a small portion of your money yourself as you believe you would be really good doing it. If you're clever or smart or resourceful, you can do just about anything yourself. It may provide you a sense of satisfaction to be self-reliant whether you decide to perform your own home improvements, put highlights in your hair or treat your own medical symptoms there are plenty of people that do these tasks every day. The question is when do you DIY and when do you work with professionals? Is some combination of the two the best route to take or should it be one or the other?

When you wake up with a sore throat, chances are you're going to start with some hot tea and honey or throat lozenges before picking up the phone to make an appointment with your primary care provider. There are some well-known remedies for a sore throat and a quick Google search will yield more options than most people would care to consider. Although you may not be a medical professional, trying to cure a minor sore throat may be a good time to be a Do It Yourselfer. On the flipside, if you suddenly are having chest pain, this is when it's best to work with the professionals and not spend precious seconds searching the Internet for cause and solutions. There will always be people who want to do it themselves but if they miss something they could end up in some hot water. Like everything there are pros and cons to the DIY approach and if you want to do some part of your financial plan yourself, talk that over with your advisor as well.

Can I Manage My Own Money?

When it comes to managing your money do you have to use a professional? The answer is "it depends" but there are plenty of things you can do yourself if you're so inclined. There are two major problems to investing your own money: Knowledge and Emotion.

You Don't Know What You Don't Know

The primary reason most people rely on a professional when investing their money is that they're unsure where to start, what they should do and if they're doing it correctly. If you have a lot of questions, that's a good sign. It's extremely dangerous to think you can read an article or watch a YouTube video and know everything you need to know about investments.

An example of when you may want to manage your own money is when you know a company you absolutely want to invest in. Instead of having your advisor manage this account, you could do it yourself. If you're going to give your advisor instructions like buy ABC stock at 55.15 and sell it at 57.98, it's probably cheaper for you to open your own personal brokerage account for this type of transaction. On the other hand, if you just like ABC company and think it could be fun and profitable to own some stock this is when it's probably advantageous for you to use a professional. Your advisor should have access to more information than you and may have a better understanding of a good strike price. (A strike price is the price you buy or sell a stock as opposed to a market price which is buying or selling at whatever the market is right that very split second.) Your investment advisor may hedge your stock pick with options and employ tax harvesting strategies to save you on capital gains tax. There are a number of techniques advisors can employ that the typical consumer is not aware of when it comes to investing.

Emotional Investing

Generally speaking people care about keeping their money and want it to grow. Excitement, greed, anxiety, desperation and hope are all factors that do not belong in your investment decisions. While there are exceptions, it's difficult to buy and sell your own investments based purely on factual decisions and not using your feelings or "gut" to make your moves.

Trading psychology has many different phases as the market goes through its up and down cycles. The average investor makes buys when it's late in the cycle and the investment has already almost peaked. As the investment goes up, excitement and greed kick in and they don't take their gains. Choosing a fixed gain or loss that you're happy with is the best way to do your investing. If you decide you're not comfortable with more than a 15% loss, provide instructions that when your investment drops 15% you sell at the loss. Too often, investors will chase a stock because they believe it will turn around and they miss out on buying opportunities because their capital is tied up. Creating buy and sell goals prior to investing will help with the emotional roller coaster

A great resource for additional information is Dalbar's Quantitative Analysis of Investor Behavior. The QAIB should be reviewed for further in-depth analysis of investment but the report cites numerous causes for poor decision making including: Loss Aversion, Narrow Framing, Anchoring, Mental Accounting, Diversification, Herding, Regret, Media Response and Optimism.

Decide Your Management Style

In summary, this is your plan, your life and your financial goals so you will need to decide what is best for your current situation. Remember that the mistakes you make will result in a hit to your portfolio. There are no mulligans for people who didn't know what they were doing or really believed an investment was going to work out. If you plan on doing some investing on your own, have a plan before you get started. Having specific entry and exit points will help with the emotional side of investing. Consult with your tax professional to confirm you're making the most of the way your investment is treated from a tax perspective. Most importantly, do research from reliable sources.

What To Invest In

Unless you're in an investment with a guaranteed or fixed rate of return, it is important to understand the anticipated returns of investments, the fees associated with the investment, tax treatments, time horizon and use of investment. Knowing the answers to these questions prior to participation will prevent confusion in the future.

For example, a ROTH is a great vehicle for investing when used correctly. However with the investment limits, the income restrictions and the withdrawal restrictions, it is important to use the ROTH as just a small portion of your overall retirement income strategy.

Please note that the information in this section is to be considered for general overall educational use and not a guarantee because in the fast-paced world of finance laws change, products change, regulations change and it is important to read the fine print of any type of investment you choose prior to your signature and execution.

How to Calculate Annual Returns

The best way to evaluate the performance of your investments is by using percentage return. Keeping an eye on the percentage rather than looking at a dollar amount allows you to compare results even when the amounts you invest are very different. You can calculate percentage return by dividing the total return by the investment's initial cost.

Annualized return or the annual percentage yield, considers the amount of time you've held an investment. Another way to make a meaningful comparison among investments, annualized return is calculated by dividing percentage return by the number of years in question.

As an example if you purchase a stock that does not pay dividends at $21 a share and sold it for $29 a share, your return will be $8. If you held the stock for one year, that would be a 38% annual percentage return ($8/$21=0.38 or 38%). However if you held the stock for four years before selling it at $29 a share, your annualized return would be 9.5% (38%/4=9.5%).

Bear in mind that inflation, transaction fees and taxes typically erode the total return on investments. Real return represents the purchasing power of what you receive from your investments, after factoring in inflation.

What Returns to Expect in the Stock Market

The Standard & Poor's 500 stock index is the bellwether benchmark that tracks the 500 largest stocks in the U.S. Most people today recall the 2008 financial crisis which caused a drop because of the subprime mortgage crisis where the S&P 500 showed a drop of -37% at the end of the year.

End of Year Returns for S&P 500 for 2005-2015

Year	Return
2005	4.91%
2006	15.79%
2007	5.49%
2008	-37.00%
2009	26.46%
2010	15.06%
2011	2.11%
2012	16.00%
2013	32.39%
2014	13.69%
2015	1.40%

If you look at an average return over the past ten years from 2005 to 2015, even taking into consideration the -37% in 2008, the average return is 8.75%.

For further consideration, the average returns for the previous decade from 1995-2004 the average return is considerably better at 14%. Below is the

End of Year Returns for S&P 500 for 1995-2004.

1995   37.58%

1996   22.96%

1997   33.36%

1998   28.58%

1999   21.04%

2000   -9.10%

2001   -11.89%

2002   -22.10%

2003   28.68%

2004   10.88%

The overall average return over the period is 11.25%, with a range of a tremendous gain in 1995 of 37.58% and the aforementioned loss in 2008 of -37%.

2006	2007	2008	2009	2010	2011	2012	2013	2014	2015	2016 to date
Emerg mkt shrs 28.8%	Emerg mkt shrs 33.6%	Govt bonds 10.2%	Emerg mkt shrs 62.8%	Commodities 16.8%	Emerg mkt bnds 9.2%	Junk bonds 19.6%	US shares 32.4%	US shares 13.7%	Devel mkt shrs 2.6%	Govt bonds 4%
Devel mkt shrs 16.1%	Commodities 16.2%	Cash 6.9%	Junk bonds 53.4%	US shares 15.1%	Govt bonds 6.3%	Emerg mkt bnds 18%	Devel mkt shrs 29.6%	Devel mkt shrs 10.4%	Emerg mkt bnds 1.8%	Inv grade bnds 5.0%
US shares 15.8%	Govt bonds 10.6%	Inv grade bnds 3.6%	FTSE 100 27.3%	Junk bonds 14.8%	Inv grade bnds 6.1%	Emerg mkt shrs 17.4%	FTSE 100 18.7%	Emerg mkt bnds 6.2%	US shares 1.4%	Cash 0.1%
FTSE 100 14.4%	Mixed portfolio 8.4%	Emerg mkt shrs -9.7%	Devel mkt shrs 26.5%	Emerg mkt shrs 14.4%	Junk bonds 3.1%	Devel mkt shrs 16.4%	Junk bonds 7.3%	Emerg mkt bnds 5.6%	Cash 0.7%	Emerg mkt b -1.1%
Junk bonds 13.7%	FTSE 100 7.4%	Mixed portfolio -13%	US shares 26.5%	FTSE 100 12.6%	US shares 2.1%	US shares 16%	Emerg mkt shrs 3%	Inv grade bnds 1.6%	FTSE 100 -1.3%	Mixed portf -1.4%
Emerg mkt bnds 10.5%	Inv grade bnds 6.7%	Junk bonds -26.9%	Emerg mkt bnds 25.9%	Emerg mkt bnds 11.8%	Cash 1.2%	Inv grade bnds 11.2%	Mixed portfolio 2.4%	Mixed portfolio 1.6%	Inv grade bnds -2.6%	Junk bonds -2.5%
Mixed portfolio 9%	Emerg mkt bnds 6.5%	FTSE 100 -28.3%	Mixed portfolio 21.7%	Devel mkt shrs 10.6%	Mixed portfolio 0.3%	FTSE 100 10%	Cash 0.5%	FTSE 100 0.7%	Junk bonds -2.7%	Commodities -3.9%
Inv grade bnds 7.2%	Cash 6.1%	Commodities -35.6%	Inv grade bnds 19.1%	Mixed portfolio 7.5%	FTSE 100 -2.2%	Mixed portfolio 8.7%	Inv grade bnds 0.3%	Cash 0.6%	Govt bonds -3.3%	Emerg mkt s -6.2%
Govt bonds 6.4%	US shares 5.5%	US shares -37%	Commodities 18.9%	Govt bonds 5.9%	Devel mkt shrs -5%	Govt bonds 1.8%	Govt bonds -4.3%	Junk bonds 0%	Inv grade bnds -3.6%	FTSE 100 -8.8%
Cash 4.8%	Devel mkt shrs 5.2%	Devel mkt shrs -38.3%	Govt bonds 2.6%	Inv grade bnds 5.6%	Emerg mkt bnds -12.5%	Cash 1.4%	Emerg mkt bnds -6.3%	Emerg mkt shrs -0.5%	Emerg mkt shrs -5.4%	US shares -9.1%
Commodities 2.1%	Junk bonds 3.2%	Emerg mkt shrs -45.7%	Cash 2.2%	Cash 1%	Commodities -13.3%	Commodities -1.1%	Commodities -9.5%	Commodities -17%	Commodities -24.7%	Devel mkt sh -10.1%

The above infographic gives an example of the market fluctuation over the past 10 years which is why portfolio diversification is essential for consistent returns. For those people who want to just stick their money under the figurative mattress, take a look at how cash has performed in this low interest rate environment.

As you can see there's a wide spread for gains and loss which is why it is essential to have buy/sell goals and to stick with them and not allow emotions to rule your decisions.

Investments and Taxes

It is important to understand the basic categories of tax treatments for investments. Let's start with the basics – just to eliminate confusion and go from there.

Many retirement investments are made with PRE-TAX DOLLARS and most other investments are made with AFTER-TAX DOLLARS. The phrase pre-tax dollars is tossed around frequently by financial professionals but often it is not fully understood by the beginner investor. In the US you pay taxes on your income. What your income tax bracket is will vary on many things but you will pay some type of tax on the money you earned while working.

For this example, we will say that Joe just earned $1,000.00 in his paycheck for the first week of the year. Since it's the beginning of the year the first amount of money he earns will be taxed at the 10% tier. We will pretend Joe lives in a state where there are no state income taxes like Alaska, Florida, Nevada, South Dakota, Texas, Washington and Wyoming (Currently New Hampshire and Tennessee don't have income tax on wages but you do have to pay taxes on income from dividends and investments). So if nothing but Federal taxes were taken out of Joe's $1,000.00 paycheck, he would end up with $900.00. If he were to put $100.00 of after tax dollars into an investment he would be left with $800.00.

$1,000.00 * 10% Federal Tax Bracket = $100.00

$1,000.00 - $100.00 = $900.00

$900.00 - $100.00 investment = $800.00

After tax dollars simply means it is what you're left with after paying your taxes. Pretty straightforward. Pre-tax dollars is a little different and can sometimes be advantageous. Generally speaking the only investments that use pre-tax dollars are for retirement. There are other pre-tax items like an employer sponsored health plan that is taken out before taxes but those are not considered investments. So in the previous example, Joe wanted to make a $100.00 investment with his $1,000.00 paycheck and was left with $800.00. In this example we will show what it looks like if Joe was to invest with pre-tax dollars.

$$\$1,000.00 - \$100.00 \text{ Pre Tax Investment} = \$900.00$$

$$\$900.00 - 10\% \text{ Federal Tax Bracket} = \$90.00$$

$$\$900.00 - \$90.00 = \$810.00$$

As you can see, Joe had $10.00 more with his pre-tax investment than his after tax investment. In this example, at the lowest tax bracket, the savings isn't significant. When you're in the highest tax brackets in excess of 35%, being able to leverage your money with pre-tax dollars can be a smart move.

There are limits and downsides to investments using pre-tax dollars. The typical employee who is investing in an employer sponsored 401K plan currently has a limit is $18,000.00. There are exceptions and you should consult your tax professional but for your average person under 50 the limit is $18,000.00.

Now that pre-tax dollars and after-tax dollars has been explained as ways to purchase investments, it is important to understand how different types of investments are taxed.

While it may not seem fair and may even be a little confusing, not all investments are taxed the same and some are taxed while the money is growing but you haven't taken a cent yet! There are some types of investments where you personally saw a loss but you may still owe taxes on a gain. This is another reason consulting a financial professional that knows how investments are taxed is a good idea.

Taxes on Stocks

If you own stocks outside a tax-sheltered retirement account like an IRA or 401k there are two ways you can be taxed. If your stock pays dividends you will pay 15-20% taxes (depending on your tax bracket) on the dividend at the end of each year.

Per the IRS website: "Almost everything you own and use for personal or investment purposes is a capital asset. Examples include a home, personal-use items like household furnishings, and stocks or bonds held as investments. When you sell a capital asset, the difference between the adjusted basis in the asset and the amount you realized from the sale is a capital gain or a capital loss."

When you sell a stock you will pay taxes on the profit of the sale. Your capital gains tax is also dependent on your tax bracket but it is typically 15% except for high income earnings at which time it will be 20%. There are exceptions to this and it is important to consult a tax professional to determine your tax bracket. The IRS lists these three exceptions when a capital tax rate can be higher than 20% and they are as follows:

1. The taxable part of a gain from selling section 1202 qualified small business stock is taxed at a maximum 28% rate.
2. Net capital gains from selling collectibles (such as coins or art) are taxed at a maximum 28% rate.

3. The portion of any unrecaptured section 1250 gain from selling section 1250 real property is taxed at a maximum 25% rate.

Keep in mind this only pertains to stocks which are held for greater than a year. If you sell a stock without holding it for 12 months, the capital gains is taxed as ordinary income which in 2016 that ranges from 10% to 39.6%. See the chart below for further information.

2016 federal income tax brackets

Tax rate on ordinary income	Single		Tax rate on qualified dividends and long term capital gains
	Over	to	
10%	$0	$9,275	0%
15%	$9,275	$37,650	0%
25%	$37,650	$91,150	15%
28%	$91,150	$190,150	15%
33%	$190,150	$413,350	15%
35%	$413,350	$415,050	15%
39.60%	$415,050		20%
	Married filing jointly / Qualifying widow or widower		
	Over	to	

10%	$0	$18,550	0%
15%	$18,550	$75,300	0%
25%	$75,300	$151,900	15%
28%	$151,900	$231,450	15%
33%	$231,450	$413,350	15%
35%	$413,350	$466,950	15%
39.60%	$466,950		20%

Source: IRS.

In the most basic of scenarios there are two ways investments are taxed: ordinary income and capital gains. You could also say capital gains taxes are either long or short but this often confuses people. The easiest way to think about it is if your investment is less than a year it's considered short term capital gains and is taxed the same way your income is taxed. For investments that are taxed for longer than a year, the investment is taxed as capital gains which is lower than your ordinary income tax. Your capital gains tax will vary but for the majority of people it is at 15%. Currently New Hampshire and Tennessee do not have a state income tax but they do tax capital gains.

From a tax perspective there are four different types of investments to understand. Please note this is a very basic explanation to provide a brief overview of how investments are typically taxed. In the diagram below there are four quadrants: liquid money, protected investments, retirement accounts and real estate. Most people will want to have some money in all four quadrants.

The quadrant represented by the dollar sign represents liquid money. This is money you can access quickly in a 0-72 hour period. Examples of this would be cash, money market accounts, savings, stocks and mutual funds. These investments are made with after tax dollars, as the money grows you're (often) taxed and when you take it out you're (often) taxed.

For example: You buy ABC stocks with money that's already been taxed, it pays dividends, so you're taxed on that and when you sell it you're taxed on the profits. That's a lot of tax paying but it is the price you pay for having money at your fingertips.

The quadrant represented by a lock is money that is protected. There are some investments that will allow participation in the stock market but you're protected from losses. Typically insurance companies provide these types of investment vehicles. There are pros and cons to these types of investments but protected investments are often a good solution for long term planning. These investments can also grow tax free and in some cases when you take your money out it is tax free as well.

The quadrant represented by the house is for real estate. Real estate is almost always purchased with after tax dollars, as it grows in value your profits are tax-deferred and you pay taxes when you sell it. If you keep your primary home for more than two years you may be able to be exempt for up to $250,000 of capital gains tax.

For example, you buy your home for $100,000.00. You put a deposit of $20,000.00 and get a mortgage for $80,000.00. Ten years down the road, your mortgage is down to $50,000.00 and you sell your house for $300,000.00.

House Sells $300,000.00 - $50,000.00 mortgage = $250,000.00

$250,000.00 – Your initial deposit $20,000.00 = $230,000.00 capital gains

In this case, you most likely would not be paying taxes on the $230,000.00 profit. However if this wasn't your primary home or you only lived there for a short time, you would most likely owe capital gains tax on the entire $230,000.00 profit of 15%.

$230,000.00 profit * 15% long term capital gains = $34,500.00 taxes

The above example is very generic and laws change so it is best to confirm this with your tax professional for your specific situation.

The last quadrant with the arrow represents retirement accounts. With the exception of the ROTH accounts, retirement accounts are almost always purchased with pre-tax dollars. A common example of this is if your employer offers a 401K plan. Money is taken from your paycheck and put directly into your 401K. Most 401K plans are invested into mutual funds. The concept being that your pre-tax dollars can work harder for you because you're able to put more money into the investment because your income taxes haven't been paid yet.

In the past your income tax rate was expected to be lower in retirement than it was while working. That scenario isn't necessarily true today as tax rates are fairly low if you consider the overall tax rates the US has seen over the past 50 years. The advantage is, however, that the majority of employer sponsored 401K plans also have your employer matching your contributions. Free money! You put in $1,000.00 and your employer also puts in $1,000.00. If you find yourself in that situation, always try to maximize your investing power by receiving your employer's money along with your own.

The money put into retirement accounts is meant for your retirement and the government would like you to keep it there. So while it's advantageous to have money in your retirement account, having a diversified financial plan is the key to minimizing your risks in bad economic times.

Diversified does not mean having your accounts with a bunch of different companies.

Is 401k a Good Investment?

The short answer is YES! But the real answer is considerably more complicated and needs to be considered thoroughly prior to signing up for your employer's offering. If your employer offers matching contributions it would seem like this is a no brainer decision. Free money, right?

One of the problems with 401k plans is that the investment options are typically limited. Few options and often poor performing funds are what you have to choose from for your 401k plan. What's worse is that frequently it's the Human Resources person helping new employees choose the fund they're investing for their retirement plan or the default is chosen which is a target-date fund. If you find yourself auto-enrolled in a target date fund, analyze the asset mix and choose one that is similar with a lower management fee. Because these fund are programmed for auto-balancing the employee typically pays a premium fee.

Why do employers have such poorly managed 401k plans? What's their incentive? The example I like to give to my clients is if I as a financial advisor managed a portfolio and did a poor job, eventually the client will (or should) take their business elsewhere. However, I have yet to hear of an employee changing jobs because the employer's retirement portfolio performed poorly. Because an employer's 401K offering is primarily used as a fringe benefit and a reason to attract and retain employees and not as a reason to seek out employment at this employer, often the employer's main concern is cost and maintenance.

Employer matching contributions have caveats. Some plans require the employee to work for the firm for a period of time (typically 90 days to 1 year) before offering matching. While other plans require a period of time (1-5 years) before you're fully invested. If you leave before the vesting time is satisfied, some or all of those contributions could vanish.

Employers have several incentives to offer a 401K plan to their employees but none of them are based on performance of the portfolio. Costs are almost always passed on to the employees and are often greater than 1% regardless of performance.

In most cases, funds invested in a 401k are not protected and do not offer a fixed rate of return. As many soon-to-be retirees discovered in 2008, their exposure to the stock market saw a loss of up to 50% and they did not have the necessary time horizon to make this up. These people are now semi-retired or had to delay retirement because of their investment returns.

Employer Contribution Scenarios

Another consideration for investing in your 401k plan is the amount of money you're investing. The general rule of thumb for determining how much to contribute to your employer matching 401k is to put in the minimum amount of money to receive the maximum amount of contribution from your employer.

For example, a common scenario for employer contribution is a matching 6%. To make the math easy we will assume the employee makes $100,000. The employee would contribute 6% of pre-tax dollars totaling $6,000 and the employer would match an additional 6% of pre-tax dollars for an additional $6,000 which would provide a $12,000 contribution over the course of a year. In 2016, the maximum tax-deferred contribution for 401k plans is $18,000 meaning the example employee can still contribution an additional $6,000.

Using the above example of a $12,000 contribution per year for 20 years ($240,000), if the investment grew at a 6% return it would provide a pre-tax income of approximately $2,200 a month. What will the cost of living be 20 years from now? What will the ordinary income tax rate be 20 years from now? While we don't know the answers to those questions we can safely say that a person accustomed to living on a $100,000 salary in today's dollars, it is fairly easy to determine that going from a pre-tax income of $8,300 a month to $2,200 a month is going to uncomfortable to say the very least.

Another common contribution scenario is the employer will decrease the contribution after a certain amount. For example, they will provide 6% matching up to $3,000 and then the contribution will decrease to 3%. In the example of the $100,000 employee, at 6 months they will have reached the maximum the employer will offer at 6% matching and then decrease to 3%. This means that for the first six months of the year the employee will have 6% matching and the remainder of the year it will drop to 3% bringing the total employer contribution to $4,500 instead of the aforementioned $6,000 of pre-tax dollars. If the employee elects to keep their contribution the same, the amount contributed will decrease from $12,000 for the year to $10,500. Should the employee also drop their contribution at the 6 month mark to 3% of pre-tax dollars the overall contribution would further drop to $9,000 for the year.

The overall annualized return in a 401k may only be between 2-4% once management fees are factored into the equation. Because of the fees associated with the management of employer sponsored 401k plans and the limited selection of funds, it is often a good idea to rollover your 401k to an IRA plan once you have left that employer. The benefit of an IRA is the possibility of better performing funds, more options and often lower management fees.

Penalties and Restrictions of 401k Plans

The great thing about 401k plans is that they're funded with pre-tax dollars so more money can be working for you. Leveraging your money should be done every time it the reward outweighs the risk. In the example of a 401k plan, you are leveraging your money because you have not yet paid taxes on it and you are expecting that a long term hold will be beneficial if the tax rate you're paying today is close to the same as it will be when it is time to withdraw that money. As mentioned previously, there is no way to know what the tax rates will be 10, 20 or 30 years from now or whenever it is time for you retire.

As the chart below indicates, the highest income brackets have had a huge range over the past 70 years. The US has also had as many as 32 different tax brackets compared to 7 tax brackets since 2013.

Year	Brackets	First Bracket	Highest Bracket	Income	Inflation Adjusted	Reason
1941	32	10%	81%	$5,000,000	$80,400,000	World War II
1942	24	19%	88%	$200,000	$2,900,000	Revenue Act of 1942
1944	24	23%	94%	$200,000	$2,690,000	Individual Income Tax Act of 1944
1946	24	20%	91%	$200,000	$2,430,000	-
1964	26	16%	77%	$400,000	$3,050,000	Tax reduction during Vietnam war
1965	25	14%	70%	$200,000	$1,500,000	-
1981	16	14%	70%	$215,400	$561,000	Reagan era tax cuts
1982	14	12%	50%	$85,600	$210,000	Reagan era tax cuts
1987	5	11%	38.50%	$90,000	$187,000	Reagan era tax cuts
1988	2	15%	28%	$29,750	$595,000	Reagan era tax cuts
1991	3	15%	31%	$82,150	$143,000	Omnibus Budget Reconciliation Act of 1990
1993	5	15%	39.60%	$250,000	$410,000	Omnibus Budget Reconciliation Act of 1993
2003	6	10%	35%	$311,950	$401,000	Bush tax cuts

2011	6	10%	35%	$379,150	$399,000	-
2013	7	10%	39.60%	$400,000	$406,000	American Taxpayer Relief Act of 2012

Source: Wikipedia

The highest US tax bracket was during World War II when the first or lowest tax bracket was 23% and the highest was 94%. The world was a different place then and our history lessons taught us what our nation did in order to survive the war. During the Regan administration taxes were simplified and the brackets dropped to as low as only 2 tiers with a top tax rate of 28%. So while the 2016 highest tax rate is 39.6% is considerably higher than in 1988 when it was only 28% many tax professionals still consider our tax rate to be relatively low. So while using pre-tax dollars to invest for your retirement is often a sound decision for people, what the tax rate will be upon retirement should always be a consideration and it yet another prime reason for investment diversification in your overall portfolio.

The other consideration for putting money into retirement vehicles such an IRA, 401k, 403B, SIMPLE, SEP or ROTH is that this money should not be withdrawn until age 59 ½. If you overextend yourself or realize you have more money than you're comfortable with in the pre-tax dollar bucket, you will be penalized 10% for early withdrawal. In addition, if you do need to take early withdrawal from your 401k you will most likely be paying Federal and State taxes as well which will be around 20% for Federal taxes. There are exceptions to these penalties and you should consult your tax professional to see if your situation makes you eligible should this type of scenario arise.

One other small caveat for 401k and IRA retirement plans is that although you should not withdrawal money before you're 59 ½ the IRS really wants you to start withdrawing by the age of 70 ½ . This withdrawal is called a Requirement Minimal Distribution or commonly referred to by its initials RMD. Some investment companies will calculator your RMDs for you and send the checks to you automatically but many won't. What happens if you don't take your RMDs? According to the IRS, if an account owner fails to withdraw a RMD, fails to withdraw the full amount of the RMD, or fails to withdraw the RMD by the applicable deadline, the amount not withdrawn is taxed at 50%.

TYPES OF ASSETS

There are four main types of investment, known as asset classes: Cash, Bonds, Stocks and Property. There are pros and cons to each and will be discussed briefly here.

Cash

Cash investments, for example, involve putting your money in a savings account with a bank or credit union. If inflation outstrips your interest rate, your money may not hold its buying power.

Bonds

A bond is a loan to a government or company. In return for the loan, you should receive the money back – plus interest – on an agreed date.

Stocks

You can invest in a company by buying shares. In return, you may get a proportion of any profit the company makes (depending on how many shares you have). You are entitled to have a say in how the company is run, including voting at general meetings.

Property

If you buy a property and rent it out, you may get an income from the rent you charge, and then make a profit when you sell the property. Land and commercial buildings, such as shopping centers, are other forms of property investments.

Investment	Pro	Con
Cash	Relatively secure/Liquid	In the current low interest rate environment, this investment will most likely not keep up with inflation.
Bonds	Regular income	With interest rates so low, bonds have lower payouts. The bond issuer may not be able to repay on the agreed date, so you could lose some/all of your investment

Dividend Stocks	Regular income and potential to grow over time	Share prices are not guaranteed, dividends may stop or decrease, potential to lose some/all of your investment
Real Estate	Relatively stable. Rental property can provide income and potential for property to increase in value	Property prices fall. Property transactions can also take a long time, so your money is illiquid

How Are Your Investments Taxed?

It is important to understand the basic categories of tax treatments for investments. Let's start with the basics – just to eliminate confusion and go from there.

Many retirement investments are made with PRE-TAX DOLLARS and most other investments are made with AFTER-TAX DOLLARS. The phrase pre-tax dollars is tossed around frequently by financial professionals but often it is not fully understood by the beginner investor. In the US you pay taxes on your income. What your income tax bracket is will vary on many things but you will pay some type of tax on the money you earned while working.

For this example, we will say that Joe just earned $1,000.00 in his paycheck for the first week of the year. Since it's the beginning of the year the first amount of money he earns will be taxed at the 10% tier. We will pretend Joe lives in a state where there are no state income taxes like Alaska,

Florida, Nevada, South Dakota, Texas, Washington and Wyoming (Currently New Hampshire and Tennessee don't have income tax on wages but you do have to pay taxes on income from dividends and investments). So if nothing but Federal taxes were taken out of Joe's $1,000.00 paycheck, he would end up with $900.00. If he were to put $100.00 of after tax dollars into an investment he would be left with $800.00.

$1,000.00 * 10% Federal Tax Bracket = $100.00

$1,000.00 - $100.00 = $900.00

$900.00 - $100.00 investment = $800.00

After tax dollars simply means it is what you're left with after paying your taxes. Pretty straightforward. Pre-tax dollars is a little different and can sometimes be advantageous. Generally speaking the only investments that use pre-tax dollars are for retirement. There are other pre-tax items like an employer sponsored health plan that is taken out before taxes but those are not considered investments. So in the previous example, Joe wanted to make a $100.00 investment with his $1,000.00 paycheck and was left with $800.00. In this example we will show what it looks like if Joe was to invest with pre-tax dollars.

$1,000.00 - $100.00 Pre Tax Investment = $900.00

$900.00 - 10% Federal Tax Bracket = $90.00

$900.00 - $90.00 = $810.00

As you can see, Joe had $10.00 more with his pre-tax investment than his after tax investment. In this example, at the lowest tax bracket, the savings isn't significant. When you're in the highest tax brackets in excess of 35%, being able to leverage your money with pre-tax dollars can be a smart move.

There are limits and downsides to investments using pre-tax dollars. The typical employee who is investing in an employer sponsored 401K plan as of this writing the limit is $18,000.00. There are exceptions and you should consult your tax professional but for your average person under 50 the limit is $18,000.00.

The money put into retirement accounts is meant for your retirement and the government would like you to keep it there. Currently you must wait until you are 59 ½ before withdrawing this money. If you take money out before 59 ½ you, in most circumstances, incur a 10% penalty. The other drawback as mentioned previously is your tax bracket is not known

DIVERSIFICATION

Diversified does not mean having your accounts with a bunch of different companies. The most important part of a financial plan is how your money is invested. Previous sections have discussed the different types of investments, the asset classes, the tax treatments and the risks – these are all very important categories. None of this matters if everything you invest in is the same.

The problem with many inexperienced Financial professionals is that they only specialize in one area of the Investment Portfolio. To be as basic as possible four financial segments or categories are as follows: Bank products, AUM, insurance and alternatives. These categories are explained in more detail below.

Bank Products

When you think of a checking or savings account the industry term for them is bank products. These are accounts usually offered by a bank or credit union. Many have the backing of the FDIC. What the FDIC does is protect the consumer from a bank failure. The limit for most deposit accounts in $250,000 for a single owner. When receiving a large lump sum of money, during the period of time you're creating your plan, it may make sense to divide that money amongst different banks so that more of your money is insured.

In this section bank products are considered your liquid assets. Your cash. What the bank refers to as deposit accounts (checking, savings, money market). Your deposit accounts should contain enough money for 3-6 months of living expenses. You also should have a separate account for an emergency fund.

Your deposit accounts contain money that is for your immediate bills and reoccurring costs. The rule of thumb for an emergency fund is to have about 20% of your net income set aside for an emergency (new roof, a set of tires, medical emergency). With many high net worth households, they choose a fixed amount such as $50,000 for an emergency fund. Your financial professional will be able to estimate an amount that makes sense for you. The most common place for an emergency fund is a savings account or a money market account.

Money market accounts are taxed differently than a savings account albeit with interest rates so low the difference is negligible.

You will want to have a portion of your income going into the accounts that pays your bills so you will not need to constantly transfer money to these accounts. Your bills are typically a mix of fixed and discretionary expenses. When thinking of fixed expenses think of things like your housing costs, utilities, food or car expenses. Fixed expenses are all of the items that you are required to pay on a regular basis. Keep in mind, these expenses while they are referred to as fixed expenses it does not necessarily mean that this amount is a fixed amount every time.

For example: One item that is considered a fixed account would be your mortgage payment. If you have a fixed rate mortgage, your payment will be the same every month, year after year. Fixed rate mortgages do not fluctuate regardless of what is going on with the economy. Your grocery bill, on the other hand, is also a fixed expense but it is not a fixed amount. The amount you spend on groceries could fluctuate based on guests, parties, travel, illness, dietary restrictions, vacations, dining out or just an increase in grocery prices.

In addition to fixed expenses, most people have additional expenses referred to as discretionary expenses. These are items that are more related to things that are considered to be fun. These are items such as dining out, travel, entertainment, vacations, fashion, luxury items, gifts and other expenses that are not a necessary part of your life. When coming into a large sum of money or having a significant bump in income it is critical that you create a budget for your discretionary expenses.

Please note there are a number of items that straddle the fixed and discretionary categories. A decade ago having high speed internet and multiple cell phones may have only been used by upper income communities but now is almost a necessity. It is very easy to get carried away high end entertainment systems, hundreds of cable/satellite channels, NFL package, pay per view and unlimited data plans. Depending on your lifestyle needs and career these items may need to be mostly in the fixed expense category.

It is not uncommon for people who receive a lump sum of money from a sign on bonus, lawsuit settlement, lottery win or inheritance to exceed the amount of money they should spend on discretionary expenses. Creating a budget for your discretionary expenses whether it is on a paycheck to paycheck basis or on a percentage of your net worth will help keep these impulses in check. Some people favor putting their discretionary money into a low-risk liquid investment with less immediate available. This slows down impulse spending and always may have a small reward from the investment's performance.

The bank products that contain money for your fixed expenses and discretionary expenses should not be considered an investment. If you don't anticipate any cash flow problems, it is certainly fine to put some of this money into a low risk and relatively liquid investment product such as a short term CD. This money should not be invested in the stock market since it is needed on a daily basis and cannot necessarily withstand short-term volatility that you might see in a stock market investment.

This section should help explain what a truly diversified financial plan and investment portfolio will look like when handled by an experiences financial professional. In a previous chapter there was information on how different types of investments are taxed. How it is important to consider how your investment is being taxed and to diversify that tax burden throughout your investment choices. As discussed it does not make sense to have all of your money in pre-tax investments or all of your money in after tax or tax-deferred Investments simply because there is no way to know what tax rates will be in the future and how tax laws will change. FDIC insured bank products can produce some gains but in this low interest environment, they're minimal. From a diversification perspective your investments fit into the three remaining categories: investments that participate in the market, investments that are protected from the market and investments that behave independent of the market.

Investments That Participate In The Market

As discussed in previous sections there are many different types of investment vehicles. In the section discussing picking a financial advisor, it was explained how frequently people incorrectly choose to diversify their risk by working with several advisors. As mentioned previously lack of investment diversification is why multiple advisors are often not a good solution to mitigate or spread risk.

There are many ways to participate in the market. In fact there are many different markets to participate in. It is wise to participate in the market when you have an investment horizon of greater than three to five years. While you have many options to invest in the market, through many different types of investment vehicles and products, creating diversification within your investments that participate in the market is a key element.

First let's discuss AUM. This book is about using regular words to describe the financial industry but there are a few terms you make hear repeatedly and it's good to know what they're talking about rather than just nodding your head in agreement.

In the simplest explanation AUM which stands for Assets Under Management means someone is going to manage your money that's in the market. Before internet trading made it possible for nearly anyone to do stock trades, these people were called stockbrokers. Now no one really uses the title stockbroker anymore and trading is very complex and sophisticated. Titles you may hear today instead of stockbroker are investment broker, wealth manager, portfolio manager or even hedge fund manager. Some firms don't say AUM but instead refer to them SAM accounts which stands for Strategic Asset Management. Typically, the way a financial professional manages your AUM is on a fee basis. Most high end wealth management firms will not charge you a fee for buying and selling but will charge a percentage of your account.

If you're a young high net worth individual working with an aggressive financial professional, it is not uncommon for the portfolio **manager** to make dozens or sometimes hundreds of trades in a month depending on market conditions. Charges are not performed on a trade by trade basis but based on an annual fee of your overall account balance.

When looking at a typical mutual fund blend there will often be several categories within that fund stating that a percentage is in one type of the market and the percentage of another type of the market. An example of a mutual fund that is allocated across various sectors is as follows:

- 10% healthcare
- 10% technology
- 30% Pharmaceuticals
- 10% Small caps
- 20% Mid caps
- 20% Large cap

This would be a blended mutual fund which is diversified across industrial sectors and size of companies. There are numerous ways to diversify your investments in the market and is essentially limited to your imagination. Investments can be made in various parts of the world, different sectors and sizes. You can invest in an index like the S&P 500 or the Russell 2000 or multiple indexes at once. And while this diversification is critical and important to factor into your portfolio all of these would be affected by an economic downturn. Looking at the example of financial crisis in 2008 while some sectors fared better than other sectors the market as a whole was down.

Historically the market has seen many large increases and many large decreases. The one thing that is known about the stock market is that the market will go up and the market will go down. It is unknown as to when this will exactly occur and how much of an increase or decrease to expect. There are many articles, books, professors and economists that dedicate their work to predicting the market volatility. Someone will be right but they may not be right every time. Having the diversification within your investment that are in the market will help with this considerably.

The wonderful thing about having so many options within the investment landscape is that even though you can participate in the market it doesn't necessarily mean you have to buy a company's stock. Years ago the only way to invest in the market was to buy shares of a stock. This is obviously no longer the case and investing in funds or indexes will spread out your risk levels to an extent. Money that you can afford to leave in the market during an economic downturn is great money to have in the market. There are numerous opportunities to make large gains when the market is down and is something that should be part of every investment portfolio. How much diversification and what type of money you have invested in the market will depend on your specific needs and objectives.

As stated in previous chapters there are investments such as life insurance and retirement accounts that can also be invested in the market. How those Investments perform and to what extent they can be exposed depends on each individual plan and carrier.

Investments that are Protected from the Market

There are products that are available that will reduce your risk and help protect you from losses in the market. They are typically offered by life insurance companies. These investments are typically used for retirement accounts. This might be an excellent choice for you if you are requiring a fixed amount of money in retirement to draw off of for income. There are many different types of products that will allow you to protect your money but still participate in some way in the market. The common solution for this scenario would be an annuity. There are numerous books and endless information about annuities and it is likely that you know someone who has used one. Annuities are a great tool if used properly and the right annuity is selected for you. The concept of using an annuity to provide lifetime income has been used for centuries.

Not all annuities are created equal and it is important to completely understand what the pros and cons of a product is before you invest. There are some fantastic options though and should be a part of your retirement income plan. The insurance companies have created many options to add to annuities such as lifetime income, critical care, long term care options and numerous others. All of these options have fees associated with them and should be discussed with your financial professional before adding to your product. The mistake most people make is they do not understand a product correctly which is why annuities sometimes get a bad rap.

The other type of product that is protected from the market but can still participate in are some types of life insurance policies. Life insurance can be used as an investment asset class. This is a little known fact but has been used for many years among the very wealthy. There are new insurance products that are created and offered on a regular basis and like annuities should be thorough understood before purchase. It is essential to talk to an insurance producer who works with multiple carriers to determine the right type of life insurance for you if you qualify. When used correctly a life insurance policy can be one of the most useful tools in your investment portfolio. Some people use the account value of their life insurance policy to give themselves loans for things like paying for a child's college education, a wedding or other large expenses like down payments on houses. This is a very complicated product and should be discussed thoroughly with an experienced qualified financial professional before considering this option. But this vehicle is a way to participate in the market and still have some protection with the money that's being invested. The upside to having life insurance as an investment class is that it has the death benefit which makes it a dual purpose investment. Often estate plans create a type of life insurance structure that will pay off the estate taxes when the surviving spouse passes so there's do not have to worry about the taxes that are anticipated for inheritance.

Using life insurance as a way to leverage and arbitrage your finances is a secret that is used among the ultra-high-net-worth people. If you have come into a sizable fortune in excess of $10M having your estate plan set up with life insurance as a leverage tool can be quite lucrative 10 to 20 years down the road.

Investments That Behave Independently of the Market.

This book is written to be simple and easy to understand by someone with little to no financial knowledge. The common phrase that is used for these types of investments is usually referred to as non-correlated assets. This simply means that these Investments or assets do not fluctuate with the market.

For example: If the S&P 500 went down 3% today would it affect how much you pay for parking downtown across from the convention center? No. If you owned a chicken farm and sold eggs and the S&P 500 went up 5% would it change the price of your eggs? No.

There are many different types of industries that do correlate with the market or behave with the market. Having Investments that do not participate directly with the market and have nothing to do with the ups and downs that happens on a daily basis is the third and final way to have true diversification in your investment portfolio.

To an extent real estate is one of these options. Non-correlated assets such as real estate are often put together for accredited investors to invest in without actually purchasing the real estate. An accredited investor is defined by the SEC as

"An *accredited investor*, in the context of a natural person, includes anyone who:

- Earned income that exceeded $200,000 (or $300,000 together with a spouse) in each of the prior two years, and reasonably expects the same for the current year, OR

- Has a net worth over $1 million, either alone or together with a spouse (excluding the value of the person's primary residence)."

For people that qualify for alternative Investments many choose to pull their market money out during uncertain times and put more of their assets into investments that behave independent of the market. Examples of this would be purchasing multiple homes or apartments for rental, choosing to invest into an oil field, purchasing livestock or other commodities and investing in REITs.

There are numerous things to take into consideration before purchasing an alternative asset if this is something that you are qualified to purchase. There are restrictions as to how much of your net worth can be in some types of alternative investments and it is important to work with a financial professional familiar with these allocations.

There are a number of restrictions that are associated with alternative Investments because they are considered high risk and are often illiquid. If you have interest in an alternative investment it is imperative to have an advisor extremely experienced in this category investment. Many and probably even most financial advisors do not work with individuals on a regular basis who qualify for these types of Investments. Most of their knowledge is from required training and not from first-hand experience.

Once you have money diversified into three categories we discussed: money that is participating in the market, money that is protected from the market and money that is independent of the market then you will have a truly diversified financial plan. This diversification however does not protect you from loss but it will certainly increase the likelihood of steady gains regardless of economic world market indicators.

Last but not least, be skeptical of investment opportunities that seem too good to be true. Yes, there are investments where you can double and triple your money. It happens. But it is not common. A return of your investment between 6%-15% on your money is reasonable and happens constantly. If it's more or less than that range, talk to your advisor or consider interviewing a new one. If you do feel good about an investment that claims an extremely high rate of return, be comfortable with a 100% loss of that investment money – that should help you decide how much to risk. If you have $1,000,000.00 of money you want to put into high risk investments, spread that $1M over 10-20 different investments. If your advisor provides you with 20 amazing high risk investments, there's a very good chance one of them is going to hit it out of the park but there's also a good chance one of them will be a complete dud. No one is going to know which is which so diversifying will help cushion the blow of the investments that didn't go as anticipated.

DIANNA MOSES

CONCLUSION

If you have suddenly come upon a large sum of money or a sudden increase in income it is critical to realize that this money could possibly last for the rest of your lifetime and the lifetime of future generations. Careful planning and a good financial professional can mean the difference between having your money last and losing significant portions to bad investments and high taxes.

Do not be discouraged if you make some mistakes along the way as long as you learn from them. Diversifying your investments and segmenting your risk will help soften the blow of financial mistakes. Putting all your eggs in one basket as the saying goes is where people make their mistakes. If you have a comprehensive financial plan developed by an experienced financial professional or a team of financial professionals that specialize in people with your situation is one of the best steps you can take.

Relying on your relatives or friends might make you feel more comfortable from a trust perspective since this is someone you've known your entire life but it is not necessarily the right way to handle your windfall of wealth. There are dozens of stories of professional athletes or actors who let their parents or siblings or cousins help them manage their money and lost all of it. Simply because someone is well-meaning does not mean that they understand all the nuances of a good financial plan.

After reading this book you should have a better understanding of how to get started planning your financial future. Knowing that a good plan is having many different types of diversification and always paying attention to how your investments are taxed puts you ahead of the game. If you are able to select the right advisor for your financial goals you will be well on your way to maintaining your financial success.

Remember all plans are different because all people are different. If you know someone else that seems like they are in a similar situation as you it does not mean that they have the same risk profile, time horizon, tax bracket or financial objectives that you do. Along with your financial team, create your own personalized, custom plan specific to your lifestyle so that it can be managed to take care of you in the future.

In summary remember you need to have not just any old financial advisor but one that specializes in high net worth situations such as yours. People who are suddenly wealthy are targets for lawsuits and unscrupulous people. Everyone trying to get a piece of your pie. Your financial team will be able to help you with a full estate plan, putting your assets in a trust for better protection. If you've never been exposed to a wealthy lifestyle it can all be overwhelming at first. Even if you have lived a lavish lifestyle in the past and your windfall of wealth is from an inheritance or divorce, keep in mind your lifestyle before the cash may not necessarily be one you can maintain now. Remember your spending levels will dictate how long your money lasts. It is important to establish budgets or allowances right away.

What many professional athletes choose to do is create a budget for themselves and they do not go over it. The understand their career could end sooner than they'd like and want to make sure they don't overspend.

Financial Worksheets

Understanding Your Financial Attitude

Understanding your financial goals is important for your financial team when it comes to creating your financial plan. But just as important, you need to understand your feelings and attitudes towards wealth. Use these worksheets to get a better understanding of your own attitude towards money, risk and your financial goals. Doing this exercise will better prepare you for questions to ask your financial advisor and understand your own goals.

What Does Money Mean To You?

Money means different things to different people. Some people think of it as a burden because of their past financial problems. Some see it as a way to freedom from worry or they believe it will make them happy. Knowing how you feel about your money will help you and your advisory team create a plan that fits your lifestyle and ideas.

Money – What does it mean to you?

Some examples people use commonly are as follows:

Burden • Risk • Freedom • Charity • Wealth • Stuff • Trust • Knowledge • Problematic • Essential • Protection • Earned • Needed • Happiness • Deserved

Money in a word: _____

Retirement

Retirement – What does it mean to you?

For a long time retirement meant spending your "golden years" rocking on the porch next to your loved one. Now people are living longer, healthier lives and often start their own businesses once they've reached retirement age.

What is the ideal age for retirement and what does retirement mean to you? Be elaborate. Does it mean multiple houses in locations all over the world? One big house where your entire family congregates on holidays?

_____

_____

_____

Lump Sums of Money

If you have just received a large lump sum of money what is your biggest financial goal with that money? Do you want to pay off your bills and the bills of the people important to you and then spend the rest setting up for your future? Do you want to leverage the money and make it work for you? Do you need this money to last you for the rest of your life?

What is the financial goal for your lump sum of money?

High Wage Earner

If you have just started making an income of over $250,000 per year but the amount of time you will be earning this amount is unknown, what do you want to do with your income so that it last? Is your goal to have a luxurious lifestyle now and when your earning potential decreases you will find another line of work? Or would you like to live a more modest lifestyle so the money you are making now will work for you?

_____

_____

Your Lifestyle

What type of social activities or hobbies would you like to do that you were financially unable to do in the past? Do you want to belong to amazing golf courses all over the world? Do you want to have a stable of horses? If your new lifestyle will include hobbies such as weekend in Aspen or diving trips to Belize these are important to consider when creating a budget. What about charities? Is there a cause you're passionate about or would you like to factor charitable giving into your financial plan?

With your new found wealth will you be changing your hobbies or social activities? If so, how:

_____

_____

Financial Benchmarks

Like anything worth doing it is an excellent idea to have goals and benchmarks. This is especially true when talking about dollars and sense. Imagine where you'd like to see your finances this time next year. Do you want to own a different house or car? Do you want to pay off debts? What are you goals in 5 years or 10 years? Do you want to be a silent partner in a business? Do you want to start a non-profit organization? How much money would you want to see in your bank account in 20 years? Do you want to provide for your children or grandchildren? Do you want to leave a legacy?

What are your financial goals one year from now?

_____

_____

What are your financial goals 5 years from now?

_____

_____

What are your financial goals 10 years from now?

_____

_____

What are your financial goals 20+ years from now?

_____

Big Purchases

What large purchases do you anticipate in the not too distant future? Are you looking to buy a bigger home? Or a home for a relative? Do you want to buy a vacation home? Do you anticipate marriage, divorce, children, grandchildren or an extravagant trip? Think about this information for some time so your goals can materialize and you will have the money available when you want it.

_____

_____

Who Do You Owe

Aside from the debts you pay regularly like your house and car payments and other fixed expenses, how much debt do you have? List all your outstanding loans even ones from friends or relatives. Be specific on the dollar figures so you will be able to make yourself whole by resolving all these debts.

_____

_____

_____

_____

Past Financial Problems

What are the financial problems in the past that you will now be able to address because of your windfall of wealth? Do you have outstanding liens or overdue credit cards? Have you had a bankruptcy or foreclosure?

_____

_____

Special Circumstance

Do you have something in particular that your financial plan must address? Such as a special needs child who will need care for their lifetime or a family medical history that you want to be ready for with long term care. These types of concerns need to be addressed as early as possible.

_____

_____

Your Financial Priorities

What are your type three biggest priorities when it comes to your money? Are income taxes the area that bothers you the most and you'd like to reduce them as much as possible? Are you worried that your income will only last for a few years and you'd like to stretch the money out in case this happens? Is your biggest concern creating a substantial amount of money for your future? Are you worried about overspending?

What are your top three biggest financial priorities?

1._____

_____

_____

_____

2._____

_____

_____

_____

3._____

_____

_____

_____

Money Thoughts

The following questions are to give you a better understanding of your overall feelings about how you view money and the way you spend it. There are no right or wrong answers; it will however give you and your advisors some things to discuss if you or your loved ones have a habit of overspending.

Money is the ultimate status symbol	Yes	No
I want more money than I could ever spend	Yes	No
Money was always tight when I was growing up.	Yes	No
When I am broke I have anxiety	Yes	No

I don't like finding something cheaper somewhere else	Yes	No
Money controls my overall happiness in life	Yes	No
I believe in giving back and like to donate to charities	Yes	No
The only reason I work as hard as I do is for the money	Yes	No
I worry I won't have enough money to live comfortably when I retire.	Yes	No
Money controls the things I do or don't do in my life.	Yes	No
Most of my arguments are about how much things cost	Yes	No
I spend money when I'm bored or disappointed	Yes	No
The people in my life spend money faster than I can bring in	Yes	No
My kids will have an allowance so they can learn money management skills	Yes	No
When I have cash in my pocket - I will spend it	Yes	No
I worry my windfall of wealth won't last long enough	Yes	No
I get upset when I spend too much and am depressed the next day	Yes	No
I live a lavish lifestyle and don't want to downsize	Yes	No
I have lied about money to people I care about	Yes	No
I am the one my friends/family turn to when they need money	Yes	No

ABOUT THE AUTHOR

Dianna Moses is a financial advisor and certified divorce financial analyst who found her passion for the financial world early. Her work on Wall Street gave her the opportunity to live all over the world and meet people from all walks of life. She believes in treating people with kindness and respect. She created this book to help people understand some of the complex matters that come with new found wealth. Moses currently resides in Scottsdale, AZ where should founded LUX Wealth Strategies. She works with a lot of women new to wealth as well as professional athletes and their coaches all over the country. Visit her website at www.luxws.com.

www.ingramcontent.com/pod-product-compliance
Lightning Source LLC
Chambersburg PA
CBHW060409190526
45169CB00002B/820